THE BUILDING BLOCKS OF INVESTING

by Marcus Travis

Written permission inquiries can be mailed to:

Leaynad Publishing

11932 Belmont Ave

Warren, Michigan 48089

Any questions can be directed to:

leaynadpublishing@gmail.com

Use SUBJECT LINE: The Building Blocks of Investing

ISBN: 9798698868484

Published in the United States of America.

Edited by Danyael M. Cheairs, Leaynad Publishing

Introduction

When it comes to learning how to invest in the stock market, there's a lot to cover, but investing is easier than you may think. In fact, investing is quicker, easier, and cheaper than ever before! That is not to say that there is no dark side, but we will discuss how 'keeping it simple' and focusing on the long term can help you to maximize your money, and your enjoyment in life.

This is not a technical course, with terms to memorize, but rather a gentle nudge in the right direction, packed with lessons from the likes of Warren Buffet, Charlie Munger, George Soros, and other world famous inventors. Their wisdom and advice will put you in the right frame of mind to choose the right stocks for you; and remember, investing is easy!

SAVING AT LEAST 10% OF WHAT YOU EARN

The Richest Man in Babylon. Have you ever heard of this book by George S. Clason? It pounds into you the idea that the richest people in life save their money, 10% of it or more in fact. 10% of each paycheck is a great achievable goal that you can commit to start doing today.

Saving is a habit, and one that helps you to control your expenses. Invest in things that you are knowledgeable about. If you do not know what a bitcoin is, and how it works, do not buy one. As Warren Buffett says, only buy stocks that you understand.

Think in terms of what people need, what they use, the price, the future price and what factors could make the stock go up. When you buy a share you are actually buying part of a company that you can make a decision in, in some cases, if you own a certain percentage you can be on a board of directors that helps make decisions with the company.

Think about how much money you have earned over the years, and how much of it you have left. Maybe you hoped to become rich some day, but you spent lavishly on trinkets and consumption, or lost money gambling. Start where you are, and don't let time slip through your hands.

So how do you save 10% of your income? Always pay yourself first! Get into a position where you can always set aside at least 10%, and then put the rest to expenses, and a small portion to enjoyment.

Seek advice from those that are competent, and learn how to make your money work for you, by investing it. Your money will be working for you, and it will multiply. Guard your money while also seeking to increase your income.

You have to be ready for an opportunity before the opportunity comes. When you invest for the long term, you are always ready to take advantage of large spikes in the share price.

For example, if you invested $10,000 in the S&P 500 between 1993 and 2013 and left your money invested, you would end up with $58,333, a 9.2 percent annual compounded return. If you missed the 10 best days, you would end with just $29,111, a 5.49 percent return. If you missed the 20 best days, you'd have just $11,984 (a 0.91 percent return).

With the stock market, you will have the ability to sell your shares at any time and use the cash on a business deal if an opportunity comes knocking. Buying, and selling stocks in 2020 is completely free on many platforms, such as Robinhood, an investing application that you can download onto your phone now. They will even give you some free money to buy a stock just for signing up. There are no transaction fees. In general, anybody with a bank account can invest quickly and easily, although, there are ways to invest without a bank account such as mailing money orders to investment companies if they will allow you to do so.

True wealth grows slowly over time. If you are determined to build wealth and follow these principles, you will find the surest path to riches. Money, that earns money, is the way to becoming rich. Strive to become wiser and more knowledgeable. This advice is free, and tested over time; the laws of wealth are unchanging.

BEING A SHAREHOLDER

A shareholder is someone who holds a share of the company and is a partial owner of the company. Shares are offered when a company decides to let the public "buy in". An initial public offering or IPO is the beginning of this process.

What makes public companies unique is that at some point they decided to sell pieces of their company to the general public through an initial public offering (IPO). These are usually Common Stocks, which is the name for the majority of stocks on the market. These entail all of the big stock companies you have heard of such as Disney or Ford.

Again, terms are not as important as a beginner may think. When you open your investing application, you will simply be depositing money with your bank information, typing in the companies name you are interested in, and choosing how much money you would like to invest. From there, you will be able to see your money go up and down, and you'll be able to sell at any time, or buy more.

In addition to investing in a single company, you can invest in the Dow Jones, or S&P 500, which I'm sure you have heard of; these are called Indexes and are made up of a small collection of well known companies, and their averages determine if the Dow Jones or S&P 500 go up or down. The Dow Jones contains 30 companies while the S&P contains 500!

Most of the stocks you consider will be on the New York Stock Exchange, or the Nasdaq. As a side note, while reading this you should skip over any portions that confuse you. The essential thing to remember is that investing in stocks is easy, but I want to give a quick overview of some words you will encounter as you complete your introduction to buying and selling.

Stocks listed on Over The Counter (OTC) should be totally ignored because they are riskier and fall into a category we can call the dark side of the stock market. Some of these companies were delisted from the legitimate exchanges and they lack crucial oversight from the Securities and Exchange Commission (SEC).

You will want to trade during Market Hours which are 9:30 am to 4 pm Eastern Standard Time. (EST) Monday Through Friday, excluding Holidays or rare events.

Two important terms are Market Cap, and Volume. Market Cap is the total value of the company when you multiply the number of shares it has on the stock market by the price per share.

A stock's Volume refers to the number of shares that are sold, or traded, on average each day. I value Volume when looking at stocks because generally good stocks have high volume, and carry less risk.

High volume means that it takes more buying or selling for the price to move, and it indicates that more people are paying attention to the particular company. An example of a very high Volume stock is Exxon Mobil; its Volume is 40,000,000. You might want to ignore stocks with volume under 100,000.

Many companies offer a Dividend, which is when the company sends you a tiny portion of their profits. After all, you do own a tiny portion of the company. As a reminder, when your stock goes up say 2%, that means whatever amount of money you invested is up 2%, your portion of money rises and falls as a percentage, with the stock price of the company. Keep in mind, a Bull market is when stocks are going up, while a Bear market describes when stocks are generally going down. And that concludes our investigation into terms.

LEARNING FROM THE BEST

"It's obvious, but I think it gets lost in the expanding universe of mutual and index fund choices. Too many of these funds use fancy names, categories, and returns that distract from the businesses held.

The businesses drive the returns. The rest is marketing." -Warren Buffett. Warren Buffett is an American investor who is the chairman and CEO of Berkshire Hathaway. He has a net worth of over 80 Billion Dollars. Warren preaches long term investing, and the importance of thinking of stocks as pieces of business'.

The longer that you own a stock, the less risky it is. This is because it is very hard to determine if a stock will go up or down on a daily or weekly basis, and as Warren says, "anything can happen in markets."

You should think of your stocks as your savings account, and think of your savings account as your cash reserves. Its more prudent to invest your money than to let it sit around earning no interest, and in truth, long term investing has shown to be very safe, and rewarding.

What does it mean that "the businesses drive the returns, the rest is marketing?" It means that there is so much marketing, fluff advertising, and news stories that make the price of a stock move up and down in the short term. Companies are constantly putting out stories to make themselves look good, and who can blame them?

Fundamentally, It's the long term performance of the business that will determine if the share holders make money. Some people like to gamble on each little news story, betting whether or not something (in the short term) will cause a stock to go up or down. In this way, the market can bring out the worst in people. The tendency to gamble and take unnecessary risks is part of human nature. Wall Street knows it and creates products to lure the gambler in all of us.

Some people are not emotionally or psychologically fit to own stocks if they use it to gamble, or cant handle temporary loses. Long term investors shouldn't sell unless the business fundamentally changes, and they should Invest by facts, not emotions.

Warren Buffett says, "We care a lot about the price, we do not care a whole lot about the next 12 months. "If you have to keep your eye on a company and stock closely it's probably too risky to own. You should buy wonderful business' and at a price below intrinsic value. Buffett would rather buy a wonderful business at a fair price than a fair business at a wonderful price.

You should always look for great opportunities, and be ready to seize them. Luckily, in the stock market, historically there is a plethora of great business that will make money for the share holders. As I'm sure you have heard, the stock market always goes up!

So how does Warren Buffett choose which stocks to invest in? Well, he looks at the business from all angles. Warren is heavily invested in Coca Cola-has been for a long time, and hes done very well with them. He related this little observation about why its such a powerful brand. Coca Cola sells 1.8 billion servings a cola per day. If they add 1 penny to the price of their product it would amount to 6 Billion Dollars more per year. People choose stocks for many reasons, this is an example of the kind of outside the box thinking that can make your investing especially successful.

Another reason to choose a stock is based on who is managing the company. A strong CEO with integrity, energy, and intellect will always do what is best for the company and the shareholders. Reading quotes, or hearing this person speak can help you to make a determination along with researching their background.

A CEO, or even a company, does not have to be well known for you to invest in it, but it must be well known to you. You must do some research. This does not mean that you need to be a mathematician, but you need to understand the business and how it fits into the economic environment that exists, and how it may fit into the future.

Another reason researching the CEO and other top managers is important is because evidence of the future of the business often exists only as thoughts inside the heads of these individuals.

Warren's business partner at Berkshire Hatheway Charlie Munger says, "I think its in the nature for stocks to go down 50% 2 or 3 times a century." That gives you an idea of what your state of mind should be. The ups and downs shouldn't play with your emotions and interfere with your thought process.

Another rule of thumb is that in general investing should be obvious and simple. You can draw upon your own personal experiences to make investing decisions. Maybe you have had the chance to see a company up close and personal because you were a customer or an employee of the company.

You may look at a price and a chart of the stock history and say "I knew it was too cheap." Charlie read about an automotive company in a magazine and decided to invest in it as one of his first trades. He bought the stock at $1 per share and sold it at $15 per share making a hefty return. He notes that the stock eventually went to $40. He also says you don't necessarily need to diversify- "I was 99 percent sure I would do fine if i never owned more than three stocks."

That is not to say that diversifying is bad. It generally takes away a lot of risk. I have a friend in Thailand who is starting to get involved in investing and asked me for advice. I took a look at the Thailand stock market and found it very confusing as most of the information was in the Thai language. Stock charts and data were also harder to come by. The market was down due to the pandemic, and ultimately my advice was to invest in the SET100, a diversified index of 100 different companies.

If you know better you don't need to diversify, but you can. You really only need one good investment to become rich. Keep in mind that, as Charlie puts it, "no matter how wonderful something is it is not worth an infinite price." You want to buy stocks at prices that are at or below their fair value for what their actually bringing to the table now, in the future, and what the perception of their future prospects is likely to be.

The world is full of foolish gamblers and they do not do as well as the patient investors. There is no scarcity of opportunities, so don't ever feel like you've missed the boat. Be sure to change when the facts change, which may mean selling but it could mean just deciding to hold the stocks you already have in the company and decline to invest more into it as you would normally do to build your portfolio value up. You must value the business in order to value the stock, and remember, the big money is not in the buying and selling but in the waiting.

There are many reasons to buy a stock, but investing in a stock because people said you should is not a good reason. Because investing has become easier than ever, more people are involved, and they will likely try to give you advice, either to try to help you or because you investing in a certain company is in their best interest.

As world famous billionaire investor George Soros said, "Whenever there is a conflict between universal principles and self-interest, self-interest is likely to prevail." Meaning that even if someone is a great person who adheres to good principles, even they are capable of setting those aside if not doing so would harm them.

Another reason to generally not take the stock advice of others is that, as George said, "The financial markets generally are unpredictable. So that one has to have different scenarios...The idea that you can actually predict what's going to happen contradicts my way of looking at the market." Markets are constantly in a state of uncertainty, and you can almost bet on the unexpected.

Wishful thinking in looking for the next huge stock can blind you to the stocks true future. As George Soros put it, "I believe the market prices are always wrong in the sense that they present a biased view of the future." He is talking about simple human nature.

Since the stock market can move tremendously based on peoples perceptions, and peoples perceptions are often wrong, the stock prices are often wrong. Sometimes it is the most down and out stocks that have the best value, "the worse a situation becomes, the less it takes to turn it around, and the bigger the upside."

That is why money can still be made in the middle of crashes, or after some piece of terrible news that is going to impact the companies short term profits. Unless a situation is just so bad that the stock is destined for zero, eventually tiny glimmers of hope will shine through, even if you're the only one who can see them.

In that case, you could stand to make a lot of money because you'll be buying when everyone else has been selling and the stock price will be low. Everyone will start to see the light and the price will rise as will your wealth.

For some, risk taking will not pay off and they'll end up in poor financial shape if they invested all they had. Others will become rich at a fast or slow pace, but rich none the less. "If you don't follow the stock market you are missing some amazing drama," as billionaire Mark Cuban put it.

Further, billionaire Peter Lynch firmly believes that individual investors have inherent advantages over large institutions, because the large firms either wont or cant invest in smaller- cap companies that have yet to receive big attention from analysts or mutual funds, but he says, "If you made it through 5th grade you can Invest."

Price is important, but it's not everything, George Soros says, "when you're just looking at the price of something, you're not investing. I mean, if you buy something, Bitcoin for example, or some cryptocurrency, you're not looking to the asset itself to produce anything.

If you buy an apartment house, you're looking at how the apartment house does. You buy a farm, you look how the farm does." When you buy a stock, you're also looking at how the business does, and with riskier stocks in their infancy, you're looking at how it will do in the future.

Peter Lynch said that "In the stock market, the most important organ is the stomach. It's not the brain." He points out that the amount of bad news you could hear is almost infinite. The question is are you going to be able to take it, do you have the stomach to take it?

Our faith is in the stock market going up in the long term, and if you share this view then you should be able to take it. We have to ask ourselves what we are going to do in certain scenarios.

What if the market goes down 10 or 20%? In many cases the answer is you have to stay in. If this sounds like something you cant do you should take that into consideration when you are trying to determine if you want to invest and how much.

Peter Lynch managed Fidelity with great success. When he was 11 years old he was a golf caddie and heard many of the men talking about stocks, and he was influenced by their excitement and conversations. He decided to look into it and while he was a college student he bought $300 worth of stock in an airplane company that transported cargo.

When the Vietnam war broke out that company was involved in transporting supplies and Peter made enough money to pay for his University Degree. He really just analyzed what the company did and came to the conclusion that they provide a really important service. He had an edge because he saw the value before others.

You too can find value before others by putting your unique talents and opportunities to work for you. What do you see around you? What makes sense? Have you seen anything really new and special?

Peter Lynch says that you "have to define when a company is getting close to maturity, and that's when you exit. Or the story deteriorates. If the story's intact, you hold on."

If a company stops growing, there's a chance they are at maturity. If they are a good company that has shown growth and they are expanding to new locations there is plenty of room left for the stock price to increase.

He emphasizes looking at what is happening right now rather than trying to predict the future because it is just going to be very difficult to do. He said, "Maybe you're right 5 or 6 times out of 10. But if your winners go up 4- or 10- or 20-fold, it makes up for the ones where you lost 50%, 75%, or 100%." Even he has been wrong and he has had to contend with good and bad luck. Be flexible and always look at your thought process, what might you change?

His view on CEO's is a little different, he warns to, "Go for a business that any idiot can run – because sooner or later any idiot probably is going to be running it." Focus' on the earnings reports of the company.

The earnings call is a teleconference where the company discusses the financial results from the reporting period. Stocks are usually more volatile in the days before and after the earnings call because people either want to be for or against the results. The calls are usually accompanied by a press release containing a summary of the financial results.

For longer term investors It's not something you would have to worry too much about, and for the purposes of this report I'm going to continue to leave out things that are less important to you.

Peter Lynch says that "When looking at the same sky, people in mature industries see clouds where people in immature industries see pie." He means that when a company is on top of the world the danger of falling is high. Newer companies are more optimistic and have more room for growth.

One last point about growth. Growth stocks are stocks in companies that have sales that have really grown. A company like McDonalds that has already expanded to most countries may not have the same growth opportunity as a company that is currently just in the USA, or just in New York.

He warns to not think you have missed out on a company just because the price has gone way up. Perhaps it can go up way more as was the case when Peter looked at Walmart ten years in. The stock had gone up 10X and Peter declined to invest only to see the stock go up 50X. He thought he had missed out but he hadn't.

Also, don't underestimate the amount of time it could take for your vision of the companies future to come to fruition. In closing, he says to buy companies that will not go bankrupt, that have staying power and cash on hand, and "If you can't convince an 8-year-old why you own this thing, you probably shouldn't own it."

Counter-intuitively you should avoid hot stocks in hot industries. These could possibly fall when all the hype is over. A lot of times investors just pile on a stock but the reality is the earnings have to be great to justify it. Hype doesn't always equal earnings.

People might be willing to buy the stock, but are those same people actually going to use the actual product that the company sells? A big bubble will be created and it's unlikely that you'll be able to time it so that you only make money and avoid the down slide.

Investing After a Crash

Investing after a stock market "crash" can yield great results. After prices fall sharply, as they did in 2008-2009, and during the Covid-19 Coronavirus national emergency, there will be many companies that become cheaper to buy.

Some are cheaper because their business is directly impacted and revenue is likely to fall, and some fall due to panic or due to a need for investors to turn their shares into cash to get through a hard time. A lot of times during these rare events, high rollers will pull their money out of the market so that they can gather information and try to form an educated opinion about what is going on. Most of that money will come back into the market relatively soon.

The price you get during a stock market crash is likely to be lower than what you've seen for years. If it is not, It's probably because the company is one that produces a product that does better during crashes.

During the pandemic, stocks like Zoom, a virtual meeting software company thrived. Generally the market will recover after a crash. During the current crisis, there was a good 1-2 weeks period where it was obvious that markets were going to slide down, and they did.

Anyone with the ability to do so pulled out, and it was the 401k's that took the brunt of the damage. This scenario is an example of a time where you should sell until you can find the bottom of the crash and re-buy into business' that will recover or even thrive into the future.

CHARTS, THEORIES, AND INVESTING

Some people have a feel for the charts and what they mean for predicting the trends. The day traders affect the daily, and short term charts significantly.

Elliot Wave Theory says that the market moves in a series of predictable waves. Five waves show the trend. Bull markets have three impulse waves, each separated by a correction, none of which retreat to the previous low. In a bear market the opposite occurs.

Dow theory uses volume to find trends, and uses the Dow Jones average to make broad predictions about other stocks. The theory assumes that is not possible to manipulate primary trends in the Indexes. Speculators, day traders, rumors and the like can manipulate the short term prices.

In 1980 the price of silver was manipulated by the Hunt brothers. The price soared to over 50$ per ounce, and then tumbled way down after the plot deteriorated. Intraday, day-to- day and possibly even secondary movements are prone to manipulation. We will talk more about that later.

Developed by Ralph Elliott in the 1920s, Elliott Wave Theory also proposes that the market moves in a series of predictable waves. Each trend in the market consists of five waves.

In a bull market there are three impulse waves, each separated by a correction, none of which retreat to the previous low. In a bear market the trend is reversed, but following the same pattern. Within each wave there may be smaller sub-waves that fluctuate around the larger trend. Because there are so many waves and sub-waves involved, finding the core trend lines is challenging

If you ever feel fearful about your decision making, use that fear or panic to fall back on the truths you know about the market and human nature. Do not let fear drive you in the wrong direction. Instead, use it as fuel to do more research and improve your decision making.

Remember, bad does not always mean bad and good does not always mean good. The market can do a lot of things but keep your eye on the actual company and its growth potential.

Sometimes you can time your entry into a stock smartly to buy in at a low point but many times it will be wise to just get in. You might want to also consider how low you're willing to let it go down before you cut a loss. Sure, the long term is key, but if something changes with the company or it goes way down when you thought it should go up over a few months you might want to at least consider a point at which you would sell. This is especially true if other areas of the market are experiencing unusual booms.

Try to read between the lines when you hear CEO's or "experts" talking about stocks. You can pick up on body language or key words that others may not. For example, if a CEO sounds upbeat but uses certain negative words like it's "tough" or "Difficult." Investors need to focus on the fact that there are countless opportunities to be had in the stock market.

You can never miss an opportunity. Look at all of the companies, and all of the green, positive stocks every single day, and the fact that stocks in general will make investors money. The key is to seize the huge opportunities that you forecast and not make rookie mistakes that cause you to be out when you should be in. Keep your eyes on the prize, you never really know when a company is going to really take off like Microsoft, Google and so many others have done!

As mentioned, the market can react negatively to good news and vice versa. Dow Theory confirms this and explains that the market looks ahead. By the time you get some of the news it's too late to take advantage of it, but of course, if you're a long term investor you're going to reap the benefits anyway. Again, what happens on a daily basis is never an indication of the overriding tread.

Prices generally reflect all that there is to know about the technical aspects of the stock. Revenue projections, interest rate movement and the like will almost always be represented in the price already, so keep that in mind when you think you can time certain events. Rare events, or 'black swan' events are easier to make short term money off of.

During the recent pandemic crash the majority of the stocks that crashed are significantly higher two months later. The black swan theory or theory of black swan events was developed by Nassim Nicholas Taleb and is a metaphor that describes an event that comes as a surprise, has a major effect, and is inappropriately rationalized after the fact. There used to be a saying that black swans did not exist, however, when a black swan was found it caused people to reflect and think about how expecting the unexpected, and preparing, can be smart.

People are usually blinded to the possibility of these kinds of events, but they play a huge role in history. The aim of Taleb's theory is to get people to think about how to be resilient and even benefit from these rare events in a way that also lets you benefit from times of smooth sailing. Taleb also wrote "Antifragile: Things That Gain From Disorder," explaining that what is a black swan event for a turkey, is actually a positive for a butcher, and he gives tips on how to be the butcher instead of the turkey.

The theory is in line with Warren Buffett's idea that "anything can happen in markets," and Buffett has said as an example that, "markets don't HAVE to open tomorrow." This was the case for a few days after the world trade center attacks. Most hugely consequential events in history come from the unexpected, such as the rise of Hitler or the Pearl Harbor attacks.

Taleb says, "I don't particularly care about the usual. If you want to get an idea of a friend's temperament, ethics, and personal elegance, you need to look at him under the tests of severe circumstances." Because you can not manufacture these emotions in your friend you just have to assume you really don't know how he will react in certain situations. Knowing that there are certain things that are impossible to know and predict will help you in the markets by keeping you prepared mentally and financially.

To reduce risk and be protected during black swan events you should put a portion of your portfolio in extremely risky stocks. The remainder would be in safer stocks that will drive most of your returns. The idea is that these events are not thought of and such an impact that even a small hedge against them could pay off huge, and 10-15% of your portfolio in these risky options would keep you resilient if they do occur.

Also, keep in mind, these unexpected events don't necessarily have to tank your safer stocks. As mentioned, most stock have bounced back, or will bounce back over time. The gambles you take in your portfolio just provide a huge upside and in the long term will cost you very little.

TRADING AFTER HOURS OR 'THE AFTERMARKET,' AND MANIPULATION

In the old days it was very difficult for average traders to trade after the market closed. This practice was left mostly to very rich investors, but now, anyone can do it. Trades in the aftermarket will make the stock price go up or down, but importantly, the price it settles at might not be the same price it opens up at for the opening bell.

Traders will take the movement into consideration but the aftermarket is a totally different animal and can be avoided for several reasons, the biggest being that you will mostly or exclusively be investing long term. Because there are fewer people trading in the aftermarket, the price is more volatile, and a single buy or sell can have a big impact on price. On the flip side, there's no assurance that one days closing price will be the next days opening price.

Per the SEC, some firms only allow investors to view quotes from the one trading system the firm uses for after-hours trading. This can affect the price you see. There are less people looking to buy or sell after hours so there is no guarantee you'll get a fair price. The aftermarket is more prone to manipulation.

If a hedge fund has 10 million dollars to play with they can buy a stock in the pre-market to create momentum. It will appear as if the stock is having solid buying. The allusion will trick investors and they may buy into the stock thinking the chart is looking positive.

The manipulators can then enjoy the increase in the price or sell their shares all at once to create panic in the other direction, and they can bet against the stock and profit. People who choose to trade after hours need to speak to their broker if they have one and go over the policy with a fine tooth comb, otherwise you'll learn the hard way that you traded money for knowledge by making a mistake.

Another reason you wouldn't want to trade after hours is because, as mentioned, these traders are likely to be bigger, smarter investors, and you'll likely to get beat.

IN CLOSING

I believe this has driven the main points home, and the quotes from great men, and great investors will provide you with a great starting point. I hope that even advanced traders will find a piece of knowledge or it will help spark an idea and motivate greater returns.

I think that we should all pay attention to companies that we know, and that we have experience with. So often it is the things which are nearest to us that can deliver us wealth. Whether that be a company that we work for, or products and people that we believe in. Keeping this in mind can save you from going down the wrong path.

Life gives many symbols and signs, working in mysterious ways. Pay attention and you can develop strong feelings to which direction to go. There are countless stock market success stories using this idea. The opposite approach of following the tide, or taking stock picks from others is more likely to go in a direction that can hurt you. Essentially, some of your highest yielding trades just might come from the heart and not the head. This shouldn't be discounted.

Always try to improve and start now with what you have. Practice with smaller amounts if necessary and with only one stock if you must. For beginners, I hope that this has motivated you to see this as your new way of life so to speak. After all, your chances of success in the stock market are really good.

The prize for sticking to it is financial freedom, increased energy, and vitality. If you're reading this as a seasoned investor thank you for bearing with us- I wish every single one of you blessed investing.